THE CANADIAN BRASS

BOOK OF INTERMEDIATE TROMBONE SOLOS

Edited by **Eugene Watts** of The Canadian Brass

■

All Selections Performed by **Eugene Watts, trombone**

■

Plus Piano Accompaniments Only

CONTENTS
In a generally progressive order of difficulty.

These solos may also be successfully played on the euphonium.

The instrument pictured on the cover is a CB20 Trombone from The Canadian Brass Collection, a line of professional brass instruments marketed by The Canadian Brass.

Photo: Gordon Janowiak

To access audio visit:
www.halleonard.com/mylibrary
Enter Code
2026-7763-6912-7974

7777 W. BLUEMOUND RD. P.O. BOX 13819 MILWAUKEE, WI 53213

Visit Hal Leonard Online at
www.halleonard.com

To All Fellow Brass Players:

Those of us who teach and play brass instruments know what a struggle it can be to find interesting and beautiful solos for our instruments. We ourselves experienced the problem first hand in our younger days, and later have encountered the same shortage of solo material at various points in our lives when we have taught brass students. It's been an aim of ours to add to the solo repertory, and we are particularly pleased to add these collections to our library of Canadian Brass publications.

What makes a good brass solo? There is virtually no original literature for our instruments, beyond a handful of trumpet and horn concertos, before the twentieth century. So if, as brass players, we want to play Bach or Handel or Mozart or Brahms, then we must choose pieces written for other instruments to transcribe for our own. And how do we choose what to transcribe? In our opinion, vocal music offers the best solution for various reasons. The pieces are often short, which is best for a brass solo. The music is written originally to words, which makes each piece have a strong emotional content and point of view that can be very satisfying to play. Because in the broadest definition the voice could be defined as a wind instrument, the phrases and lines are naturally well suited for brass players. And further, there is simply far more solo music written for the voice than any other instrument in history. Composers seem to have been continually inspired by singers throughout the centuries, and we see no reason why we brass players shouldn't benefit from all that inspiration! After having said all of that, it will come as no surprise to state that most of the pieces we have chosen for these solo books are transcriptions of vocal pieces. Another priority in making the selections was to include mostly work by major composers from the history of music. Altogether too much of the educational solo music available almost exclusively presents work by minor or unknown composers.

The recordings we have made should be used only as a guide for you to use in studying a piece. We certainly didn't go into these recording sessions with the idea of trying to create any kind of "definitive performances" of this music. There is no such thing as a definitive performance anyway. Each musician, being a unique individual, will naturally always come up with a slightly different rendition of a piece of music. We often find that students are timid about revealing their own ideas and personalities when going beyond the notes on the page in making music. After you've practiced for weeks or months on a piece of music, and have mastered all the technical requirements, you certainly have earned the right to play it in the way you think it sounds best! It may not be the way your friend would play it, or the way The Canadian Brass would play it. But you will have made the music your own, and that's what counts.

Good luck and Happy Brass Playing!
The Canadian Brass

EUGENE WATTS was born and raised in Sedalia, Missouri (the home of Scott Joplin). Like the story of *The Music Man*, a traveling instrument salesman convinced his parents that Gene would make a great euphonium player. He soon switched to trombone and started playing in taverns and nightclubs, steeping himself in a jazz and Dixieland tradition. He worked his way through college at the University of Missouri with his own Dixieland band, "The Missouri Mudcats." Further studies followed with Arnold Jacobs. He established an orchestral career in a succession of positions with the North Carolina, the San Antonio, and the Milwaukee Symphonies, and was asked by Seiji Ozawa to become principal trombone of the Toronto Symphony. While in Toronto, his intense interest in chamber music led to the founding of The Canadian Brass. Beyond his musical career, Gene is a continuing student of transcendental meditation.

PATRICK HANSEN, pianist, has been musical coach and assistant conductor at Des Moines Metro Opera, and has served on the staff of Juilliard Opera Center as a coach and accompanist. He was assistant editor on the new G. Schirmer Opera Anthology, and has recorded several other albums for Hal Leonard. Patrick holds degress in piano from Simpson College and the University of Missouri at Kansas City.

ABOUT THE MUSIC...

Gabriel Fauré: After a Dream (Après un Rêve)

This is Fauré's most famous song, and is often played by instrumental soloists of all kinds. (Fauré himself transcribed it for cello.) It's about a lover's dream of happiness with the ideal lover, and the pain of awakening from the dream alone. Fauré (1845-1924) was one of France's major nineteenth century composers, turning out operas, piano music, orchestra music, chamber works, and choral pieces (the Requiem is well known). But more than any other composer in French history, Fauré excelled in setting poetry to music for the voice to sing, and his many, many songs are at the center of the international repertory of art songs. Fauré became the most important music professor in France, revered for decades at the Paris Conservatoire as the teacher of every French musician of worth. (Pronunciation tip: Fauré=four-AY)

Henry Purcell: Strike the Viol

For some reason, difficult to explain, in the 18th and 19th centuries there were virtually no British composers of the stature of the major composers on the European continent. Prior to the 20th century, the last world class composer from England was Henry Purcell (1659-1695). He grew up in a prominent musical family and had the training that allowed him contact with the elite musical circles. He became organist of Westminster Abbey at the age of 20, and remained in royal appointments for the rest of his short life. He composed extensively for the theatre, providing incidental music for plays and also operas. He is buried in Westminster Abbey. (Pronunciation tip: the accent is on the first syllable, PUR-sul, *not* on the second syllable, as in pur-SEL)

Jacques Offenbach: Barcarolle from *The Tales of Hoffmann*

Several countries have had their masters of operetta and musical theatre. In England there was Gilbert and Sullivan, in Austria there was Johann Strauss, in the United States there was Jerome Kern, Rodgers and Hammerstein, and dozens of others. The French counterpart for these operetta composers was Jacques Offenbach (1819-1880). For some time he earned his living as a cellist in Paris, but later rose to conductor. In the mid 1850s he began producing his own works in a theatre he had rented himself, having failed to find any opera or theatre company to produec his operettas. He was wildly successful, and became the toast of Paris, producing show after show for two decades. Toward the end of his life his greatest ambition was to compose a full-fledged opera, and he had largely completed the task when he died in 1880. A friend completed the opera for him, and it was premiered that same year. *The Tales of Hoffmann* has remained a favorite on the world's opera stages ever since. The "Barcarolle" opens act II, set along the canals of Venice. By the way, Offenbach is the composer of the famous "Can-can." (Pronunciation tip: Offenbach: OFF-en-bock)

Richard Wagner: The Evening Star from *Tannhäuser*

Richard Wagner (1813-1883) was, after Beethoven, the most powerful and influential composer in European music of the 19th century. (And he didn't hesitate to explain that fact to anyone and everyone!) An undeniable genius, a megalomaniac, author of radical political literature, and prone to excessively indulge every excess, it's impossible to overstate Wagner's influence over the artistic climate and trends of Europe from about the year 1850 until well after his death. His music was dramatically different from all before it, becoming dissonant and bold, using the orchestra and voices heroically and with a grand sweep that had never before been heard, evoking his beloved legends and myths of pre-Chritian Germany. The man and his music inspired either fierce loyalty or vehement attacks, but by the 1870s his followers far outnumbered his detractors, and nearly every composer of every nationality in Europe was influenced by him for the next fifty years. *Tannhäuser*, first performed in 1845, is among his earlier works. (Pronunciation tips: Wagner=VAG-nr, Tannhäuser- TAWN-hoy-zr)

Franz Schubert: Serenade (Ständchen)

Schubert (1797-1828) was the first master of German song literature, or *lieder*. He composed over 600 songs for voice and piano during his lifetime, all of which are settings of German poets of his time (or occasionally German translations of other European poets). But his talents were not confined to songs alone, and he wrote a wide variety of music, for piano, for orchestra, for chamber ensembles, for choruses, and operas for the stage. He was "Bohemian" in nature, an artistic dreamer who had little money, and was principally supported by the wide circle of friends who admired his talents. The very beautiful "Serenade" is just that, a lover standing in the moonlight, singing for his love to come down from her window into his arms. (Pronunciation tip: Schubert=SHU-bayrt)

Charles Gounod: The Page's Aria from *Faust*
Valentin's Aria from *Faust*

Charles Gounod (1818-1893) was the most successful opera composer in France in the mid-19th century. Indeed, behind *Carmen, Faust* is the most popular French opera of all time. It is loosely based on the story by Goethe of the man, Faust, who sells his soul to the devil to attain a woman, wealth and power. (It might sound like a good deal, but trust me—it isn't.) Gounod wrote many other operas, but never again achieved the success of *Faust,* which was premiered in Paris in 1859 In the plot, the page, Siebel, is in love with Marguerite. While in the garden, he sings to the flowers to greet her with his love. Regarding the second aria, the soldier Valentin, Marguerite's brother, must leave for the war. Before he goes, he reflects on the sadness of leaving home and family, the glory of battles to come, and prays that God will protect his sister until his return. (Pronunciation tips: Gounod=goo-NOH)

Gilbert and Sullivan: The Pirate King from *The Pirates of Penzance*

The great English operetta creators, Gilbert and Sullivan, were the Rodgers and Hammerstein of their day, creating the equivalent of Broadway musical comedies for London of the 1880s and 1890s. Arthur Sullivan wrote the music and W. S. Gilbert wrote the witty and politically satirical words. Their shows, such as *H.M.S. Pinafore, The Mikado,* and *Pirates of Penzance,* are still very popular. It's interesting that though celebrated and successful in their collaboration, Sullivan and Gilbert never particularly liked one another, and had public battles on more than one occasion.

Wolfgang Amadeus Mozart: Figaro's Minuet from *The Marriage of Figaro*

The Marriage of Figaro started out as a politically charged comedy by playwright Beaumarchais in the years leading up to the French revolution. The play is a scathing attack on the authority of the aristocracy, and the "victory" (in dramatic terms) of the servants. It was banned in most of Europe, including Vienna, where Mozart lived. Through some persistent persuasion, and also by avoiding some of the play's sharper points, Mozart and his collaborator, librettist Lorzeno da Ponte, were given permission to proceed with writing the opera based on the play. It was premiered in Vienna in 1786. Figaro is servant to Count Almaviva. In this minuet, he mockingly sings of his complete obedience to his master. Then in a stormy middle section, he tirades against the Count's random authority. (Pronunciation tip: Wolfgang=VOOLF-gahng, Amadeus=Ah-mah-DAY-us, Mozart=Moat-zart).

Scott Joplin: Solace

Scott Joplin (1868-1917) is universally recognized as the most accomplised master of the Ragtime style. Considering this, it's difficult to believe that for most of this century his music languished in obscurity. Joplin's piano pieces were popular during his lifetime, but soon after his death in 1917 his music fell out of the repertory. One can't help but believe that if he had lived just a decade longer, more into the mature recording age, that it would have been a different story. But works of high caliber usually do not go unnoticed forever. The Joplin revival began in the 1970s, and since that time (particularly after the hit movie "The Sting") his music has been played and loved all over the world. "Solace," written in 1909, is one of Joplin's most elegant rags for piano.

Arcangelo Corelli: Preludio

Corelli (1653-1713) was not a prolific composer, yet his small output was significant enough to influence instrumental composition in Italy and beyond to other parts of Europe. He was one of the first composers to fully develop advanced music for instruments. (Prior to his time music had been largely vocal; when instruments were played, they most often accompanied voices.) Stylistically, his music was quite original in its time.

Gaetano Donizetti: Cavatina from *Don Pasquale*

Donizetti (1797-1848) was one the principal popular composers of Italian opera in his day, and in the span of less than thirty years wrote nearly seventy complete operas (more than anyone else in history), besides hundreds of other compositions. Historians have also discovered many thousands of letters written by Donizetti, and between his composing and letter writing, one wonders how he ever had time for anything else! (The poor man literally drove himself crazy, and died mentally deranged.) Don Pasquale is a light comic opera from 1843. (Pronunciation: Donizetti=do-nee-TSEHT-tee)

AFTER A DREAM
(Après un Rêve)

Gabriel Fauré

STRIKE THE VIOL

Henry Purcell

BARCAROLLE
from
THE TALES OF HOFFMAN

Jacques Offenbach

THE EVENING STAR
from
TANNHÄUSER

Richard Wagner

SERENADE

Franz Schubert

THE PAGE'S ARIA
from
FAUST

Charles Gounod

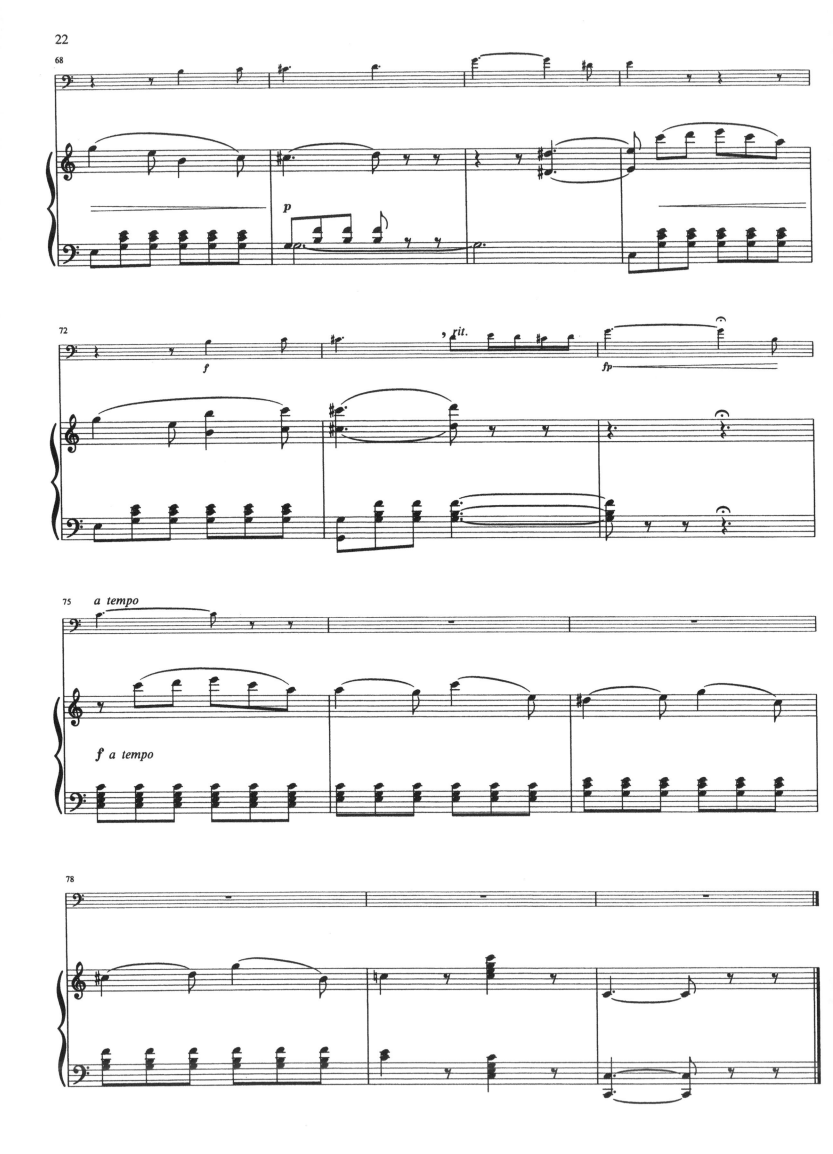

VALENTIN'S ARIA

from
FAUST

Charles Gounod

THE CANADIAN BRASS

BOOK OF INTERMEDIATE TROMBONE SOLOS

Edited by **Eugene Watts** of The Canadian Brass

■

All Selections Performed by **Eugene Watts, trombone**

■

Plus Piano Accompaniments Only

CONTENTS

In a generally progressive order of difficulty.

These solos may also be successfully played on the euphonium.

7777 W. BLUEMOUND RD. P.O. BOX 13819 MILWAUKEE, WI 53213

Copyright © 1992 HAL LEONARD CORPORATION
International Copyright Secured All Rights Reserved

Visit Hal Leonard Online at
www.halleonard.com

AFTER A DREAM
(Après un Rêve)

TROMBONE

Gabriel Fauré

STRIKE THE VIOL

TROMBONE

Henry Purcell

4

BARCAROLLE
from
THE TALES OF HOFFMAN

TROMBONE

Jacques Offenbach

THE EVENING STAR
from
TANNHÄUSER

Richard Wagner

TROMBONE

SERENADE

TROMBONE

Franz Schubert

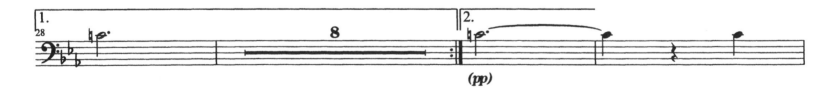

THE PAGE'S ARIA
from
FAUST

Charles Gounod

TROMBONE

VALENTIN'S ARIA

from
FAUST

Charles Gounod

TROMBONE

8

TROMBONE

THE PIRATE KING

from
THE PIRATES OF PENZANCE

TROMBONE

Words by W.S. Gilbert
Music by Arthur Sullivan

Repeat optional

FIGARO'S MINUET
from
THE MARRIAGE OF FIGARO

Wolfgang Amadeus Mozart

TROMBONE

TROMBONE

SOLACE

TROMBONE

Scott Joplin
Arranged by Rick Walters

Repeats are optional throughout.

TROMBONE

PRELUDIO

TROMBONE

Arcangelo Corelli

CAVATINA
from
DON PASQUALE

Gaetano Donizetti

TROMBONE

THE PIRATE KING

from

THE PIRATES OF PENZANCE

Words by W.S. Gilbert
Music by Arthur Sullivan

Repeat optional

FIGARO'S MINUET
from
THE MARRIAGE OF FIGARO

Wolfgang Amadeus Mozart

SOLACE

Scott Joplin
Arranged by Rick Walters

Repeats are optional throughout.

PRELUDIO

Arcangelo Corelli

CAVATINA
from
DON PASQUALE

Gaetano Donizetti